The Water Drop Connection

By: Melanie J. Hebert

This book is dedicated in loving memory of my little sister,

Lana Lynn Hebert

August 29th 1978 - January 19th 1995

When I told my friends I was writing this book, they said, "This will be very therapeutic for you."

Ha-ha!

I've been through therapy; this one's for all of you.

Maybe it will bring you a better understanding about me and the things

I've learned on my journey so far.

I love you all,

Melanie

The Water Drop Connection

Chapter One: Blinding Moments

Blind: unable to see; lacking the sense of sight; sightless. Unwilling or unable to perceive or understand. Lacking all consciousness or awareness.

It was a sound that I'd heard at least a million times the phone ringing. Its familiarity somehow slipped away, and the house was empty. The ringing was bold, crisp and seemed to get increasingly louder. I had just awoken from actual sleep, unusual for a teenage insomniac who never took naps. I don't know how many times the phone rang. Suddenly, energy and anxiety merged for a split second, and like a hovering dragonfly, I picked up the receiver.

"This is Oshawa General Hospital. Is this the Hebert residence?"

I said. "Yes."

The woman on the other end of the phone said, "Lana Hebert was in a serious car accident."

"I'm her sister. Is she okay?" I said, while in my mind, at that second, I laughed. I thought, *What an idiot! Probably broke her arm or something stupid.*

Trauma cannot be rationalized at the moment when it occurs. It's like your heart and mind try desperately to protect you from what could be the most unnatural, obscene thing, something so horrific, your comprehension fails for a blinding moment.

The nurse said, "No she's not okay. We're airlifting her to Sunnybrook." I remember the phone falling from my fingers. I watched as it fell, noticing the colour of the receiver was dirty beige. The cord was far too long for the space it was in, lying on the brown shag carpet in a tangled mess. The sound of the receiver hitting the floor with a muted thud still haunts my mind. Then, reality abruptly slapped me in the face.

I turned my eyes to my father, who was gone in an instant. I had to stay behind to make the phone calls. The hospital was only a few blocks away. I can't remember taking a single step to walk there. The January air was frigid, but my chest was burning. Through my tears and panic, I must have looked like a fish gasping for air.

I rushed through the hospital doors and into the emergency room. There, in front of me was a stretcher, surrounded by chaos. Doctors, nurses, plastic tubes, fluorescent lights, all hurriedly passed by my body. In my mind, the room moved in increments, like I was being shown moments, slow and deliberate. They were all being etched into my brain. I couldn't see her face. All I saw were the blood-spattered, white sheets and metal rails on the sides of the stretcher, reflecting those awful lights in brilliant flashes as they passed my eyes. My eyes, which were desperately searching for peace, safety, sanity, and comfort, but finding none. Then the uniforms, doctors, nurses, and curious onlookers exited through doors we hoped we'd never have to see. It wasn't she who lay there broken and lost anymore. Lana was already gone; it was I.

Patience: The quality of being patient, as the bearing of provocation, annoyance, misfortune, or pain, without complaint, loss of temper, irritation, or the like.

When I arrived at the hospital, they led me into a special room, which was pleasantly decorated with chairs that were only slightly more comfortable than the cold, hard, waiting room chairs. No matter how you dressed it up, it was still a cold, hard waiting room. I could have never imagined "Waiting Room" would become such a profound combination of words. For some of us, it became a place that would change us forever. Waiting for news of our loved ones, contemplating our lives, asking ourselves hard questions, like, did we say everything we needed to? Was I good to that person? What have I done to deserve this? What have they done to deserve this? Trauma also reveals the truth. There was no hiding or covering up when our family came face-to-face with each other. The family dysfunction might as well have been set ablaze since it was brightly illuminated as we all fell apart, none of us offering each other a soft place to fall, or any other form of solace.

Despite the perks of the "special" waiting room we were in at that moment, I had no gratitude. It was obvious there was some effort directed toward creating a warmer atmosphere and giving the families some privacy and peace, but nothing in that place mattered. I could see and feel nothing, but my own fear and pain. It was close to the chapel, but God and I hadn't been on very good terms for quite some time. A bereavement counselor came in to offer words of comfort. I laughed at her, thinking, *You have no idea what I'm going through. You didn't know her or love her. How could you even begin to think you could possibly help me?*

You're just a strange lady who is getting paid to tell me what I you think I need to hear. We were also introduced to, and updated by a brain surgeon and other specialists who spoke in a language that I couldn't understand. They tossed out a lot of medical terms, prognoses, and possible outcomes. They said they were trying to put her back together; and it all sounded so mechanical, like they were discussing a broken machine, not to mention the calmness and certainty in their approach. I wouldn't allow myself to believe things were as grave as they truly were. She had a "closed head injury," her "brain was swelling," and now she was in a "medically-induced coma."

Then, more waiting in the waiting room. When I first got the phone call, I called one of my closest friends who happened to live down the street. Sonya slept beside me at the hospital, hugged me, when my own mother wouldn't, and watched me lose everything that year. She and I were lifers. At one point, we went outside for a cigarette. I remember pacing back and forth, yelling out loud with such fury, "I don't want to tell people my sister died when I was nineteen!" There was a conflict between pure denial that this could be happening to me, while concurrently, remembering a lifetime of pitiful moments. My childhood was difficult and my teen years were not much easier. Life for me always seemed like it had been too hard. Even as a child, I always felt old and tired. Like I was just surviving, rather than living my life. As I stood there, cursing the cold, empty, night sky, all I could think was, *it should have been me. I should have protected my baby sister. It was my job, and I failed everyone.*

Pain moves in waves; it crests and breaks, but whether the peak of the wave is the most painful, or the crashing onto the rocks, I'm not sure. Whether it's rain, snow, puddles, ponds, or a great, wild river, it is all water. The news of her accident--was that the worst? Or was it when the doctor told me I needed to go in and see her for the last time, to say goodbye? Deciding I couldn't bear to see her like that, I chose not to go in. The doctor sent for a psychologist to talk to me, who warned me that if I didn't go in, I would be mentally scarred for life. I was terrified and didn't know what to do. Was this the wave crashing down all around me? My boyfriend at the time offered to go in and see her, saying, "I'll tell you if it's a good idea." When he came out, he told me if I went in, I would never forget her final image; it would be my last memory of her. I couldn't face that, but I felt so guilty and helpless. I felt like a scared little child who had grown up to become a coward. After a few days, all Lana's brain activity ended, and my parents chose to donate her organs and remove Lana from life support.

Hindsight: The ability to understand, after something has happened, what should have been done or what caused the event.

When I got the final news that she died, I was at home in my bed, with several close friends. We were joking and sharing memories of Lana, and how wild, crazy and fearless she was in life. We smoked and smoked, trying to numb any feelings that might creep in. Everyone was so scared to let me feel anything, as if waiting for me to fall apart and implode the whole universe. That wasn't me. I was always the strong one, I kept things together. I took care of that kid like she was my own. All my life, my family told me, "That's your little sister; you take care of her," and I did. I protected her from all of our family's demons and tried to shield her eyes from the ugly things I shouldn't have seen. As awful as it sounds, when I got the news of her death, I had a sense of relief, relief from waiting in limbo. Death was quick. Grief took its time.

That first week, I was never alone--phone calls and people stopping by the house with food and flowers. At first, it was sweet and thoughtful. I was grateful to have something to focus on, when every waking second, everything seemed to be slowly slipping away from me. What hurt the most about seeing people was not my pain, but the looks on their faces contorted with the pain they felt for me. That made it real. The food started piling up in heaps of labeled Tupperware containers in the refrigerator. Nobody felt like eating. I was high, Dad was drunk, my mother was somewhere in her own world, praying. We all had our own addictions. The living room was designated for flowers. The room soon made me sick. I felt like I would run out and vomit in the sink if I stayed in there for too long. Flowers covered the tables, the floor, and even the couch. They were wall-to-wall, in every color and size of flower arrangement you could imagine. And the cards! Piles of unopened cards that all said the same things; and those empty words, anybody's words, were never enough and sounded so un-healing in those dark days. It was like our house had become a funeral parlor. I hated every last bloom, every message of, "Your poor family," "poor dead girl," and "poor girl who's still here." We hadn't even had Lana's funeral, and the weight of those words, along with the flowers, were suffocating me.

I looked through my closet, wondering what to wear for my little sister's funeral. You never imagine that scenario or having to be in such a horrible reality. The last time I saw her, she was lying on the couch with her hands behind her head, propping it up. Her long legs were crossed at the ankle, and I was telling her not to ruin the shirt she borrowed, or rather stole from my drawer. She told me, I was "such a bitch" and laughed at me. The shirt was white with pink lettering that said "Million Dollar Babe." We laughed and then I went downstairs and fell asleep… until I heard the phone ringing.

I have no clue what Lana was wearing when she was buried. My dad's girlfriend carefully picked out something. I didn't want to talk about it or participate in any of the arrangements. I just wanted the day to be over and everyone to leave me the hell alone, or just leave me in my own hell alone.

I wore black. January 19th 1995. It was cold and the night before we had had a heavy snowfall that covered every branch of every tree with white marshmallow clumps. The air was still and quiet; there was no wind. The sun was bright; it really was the perfect winter day. Although it was cold, I couldn't feel it. I was losing the ability to feel anything. The funeral home was packed. The overflow room was also full. Lana was a popular girl. Everyone liked her; even her public school teachers were there. I felt so out of place and lost. Everyone I knew who cared about me and loved me looked like gawking strangers on that day. I wanted to sneak out onto the street and scream, hoping I would wake up from all of it. The service, I'm sure, was nice, but I can't recall a single word of it. It was like listening to words while being underwater, muffled and far away.

In chaos, sometimes there are moments of clarity. Three things I clearly remember about the funeral: the first was my grandfather, trying to physically drag me to the open casket, and me breaking free, while trying to explain myself. He couldn't understand me, and like the psychologist at the hospital, was fearful that this would haunt me forever if I didn't see her. *My sister is dead! Trust me! I believe you!* But it was about closure for him. I was young and still learning what that meant for me. Only you know what will bring you peace.

Second, I remember sitting in the packed room. There were so many faces and bodies, it was standing room only. I couldn't tell you who any of those in attendance were, although I'm sure I knew all of them. There were three people, however, that I knew well and recognized that afternoon. A ray of sunlight caught my eye and it streamed through the chapel, landing on my friend's family. They brought their new baby, and she was beautiful and glowing. For a moment, I forgot all about time and the horrible place I was in, and I smiled. Then the guilt of How dare I smile? hung over me. My brief respite of momentary peace instantly vanished from my grasp, replaced by overwhelming guilt and sadness.

Last of all, I remember leaving. I walked into the hall, and standing there, holding a single rose for me, was one of the boys from the car accident. It still wasn't clear what happened that night with the three of them. My sister was the only one who died. I immediately hugged him. He was one of the last people to be with her. He had the answers to my questions about her last moments, the lost moments of her life, my beautiful little sister's lost life.

In good old Catholic tradition, we trudged over to the cemetery for the lowering of the casket into the frozen ground. The casket was baby blue, like her eyes. We stood there solemnly and even with all the people standing around, I felt like it was just she and me. My grandfather gave me a rose to place on the casket. I stepped forward and collapsed in front of her blue death box in the snow on my knees. I cried and cried on the ground for what seemed like a lifetime. My boyfriend scooped me up and took me home as I wept uncontrollably.

Chapter 2: The Unraveling

Unravel: to free from complication or difficulty; make plain or clear, solve to unravel a situation, to unravel a mystery. To take apart undo, destroy.

The day my sister died, we had big plans. We were going to move out together, away from our alcoholic father, and get our own place. We spent the day exploring our options and strategized: we were going to start fresh, completely on our own, and get our lives on track. We were actually skipping arm-in-arm down the sidewalk, singing out loud CCR's "Have You Ever Seen the Rain?" Looking back now, everything about that day had an unnatural way of falling apart and we let things slip through the cracks. I now believe there are no accidents; and we are exactly where we are supposed to be, wherever we are, at all times. Once we returned home that day, I suddenly felt tired. I went to my room in the basement and fell asleep, something I never did.

The usual routine was to go downtown and visit a friend of ours. While I was asleep, two of Lana's old friends showed up at the house, out of the blue, and invited her to go out with them. The funny thing was, every time these particular guys showed up, I would usually go with them. She never woke me up that day. From what I heard, they drank beers before they left our driveway. Only the three of them truly knew what really happened that night. My friend from downtown told me he was on his way over earlier, but had company who wouldn't leave. He beat himself up for a long time, thinking what might have happened if he had only come over when he said he was going to. There were so many little events leading up to the tragedy. They made us all question our actions, saying, What if we had done this or that? Would she still be alive?

Seeking justification, I decided it had to be somebody's fault. Rumors were flying wildly about the driver being drunk and not caring. I was told he was flirting with the nurse on the way to the hospital in the ambulance. To make things worse, he never called or apologized, making him look all the more guilty. In the months afterwards, he was often seen by my friends at all the local bars, partying. He was able to attend his high school graduation that year. The longer his life seemed to happily progress, the angrier I became at him, as well as everything and everyone in *my* life. Vengeance was building inside of me. I was creating a monster out of a boy who simply made a really bad choice that day.

I started to obsess over what he had done, and the accident that took everything away from me. I planned ways to make him suffer. I dreamt about it, tasted it, and breathed it, in and out, every minute of the day. At that time, I was acquainted with a few shady characters from whom I could call favours, who would gladly fix him for good. In my heart, however, there was still some morality. I kept telling myself that since he was drinking and driving, the police and the courts would take care of him. It took a few years to get him to court, and he was never convicted of anything. He walked scot-free, even appearing in a newspaper article about the accident. They described him as the "poor boy that lost his girlfriend in a tragic accident." I nearly went through the roof and immediately called the paper to give the editor a vitriolic earful.

The thought of him continuing his life while my sister's was lost consumed me whenever I wasn't reliving the day of the accident, which I did relentlessly. I couldn't eat. I forgot things. Sometimes, I forgot to shower, or I would stay in the shower for a ridiculous amount of time, just so I could hide my tears. One day, I got into a car and instantly had a major panic attack. I was screaming for someone to let me out, and when he did, I walked home. I didn't get into a car again for over a year. I kept seeing Lana's head smashing into the dashboard over and over. It became a constant terror I'd never experienced and had no control over. I memorized every bus route out there.

When someone dies, everyone gathers around to grieve, but no one talks about how life is supposed to move on and how to help people go back to their own lives, as they should. You are left all alone. Not only have you lost someone you dearly loved, but you've also lost your former identity. I went from being "Melanie" to "that's the girl whose sister died." It hurts to see life marching on without you, no matter how hard you kick, scream, and dig your heels in. Life never stops for anyone. I felt like I would betray her memory if I experienced any joy, or made any plans to live. Happiness for me was now impossible. For me to stop feeling angry and hurt meant I had forgotten her. The truth is that our loved ones would never want us to feel that gnawing misery, but grief has its own timing. It provides opportunities for us to discover how to heal and the road toward peaceful existence.

Water the seeds of fear and they will grow like weeds, getting entangled with every part of your identity. My fear grew unabated. The chance of running into the boy who caused the accident petrified me, and I stopped going places where there could be any possibility of seeing him. No restaurants or shopping malls. I became terrified to face this person. I felt like I would be like looking into the eyes of the devil himself, and instantly die, or worse. I was not close to my family, and my relationship with them at the time was failing miserably. I began shutting out my friends too, because I got so sick of their sad faces, constantly reminding me of what happened. That benign question, "How are you?" sounded so stupid, I nearly found it insulting. I knew it was sincerely out of concern, but all I saw was how they were pestering me. I wanted nothing more than to hide from them, my feelings, my guilt, my own reflection. I wanted to escape my world, before I'd try to escape my life.

Soul mate: a person with whom one has a strong affinity, shared values and tastes.

I planned a trip to Vancouver. Everyone thought it would be better for me to get away, and it was far enough away that the fear of running into the monster was not a concern. In life, as long as our eyes are open, I believe we meet pivotal people and have relationships that provide great healing and bring wisdom to us. There were many people I met along the way, for which I am blessed and a better person for having known, not only in the lightest of times, but the darkest ones too.

Richard was a friend of the family who grew up in the same neighborhood as my parents. He went to school with my mom and they were in a band together during high school. He was a songwriter and I loved him madly from the age of ten. It was he who opened the door to songwriting for me. He said, "I'll tell you what, if you can write me a song, I'll record it in my studio." You better believe I wrote that song, and I've never stopped writing.

Richard always made everything seem possible. He wanted to be a songwriter so he packed up his family, moved to the West Coast and did it. In my young eyes, he was bold, brave, and a true adventurer. My trip to Vancouver took me from being just his childhood friends' daughter, to beginning a new and profound friendship for life. We talked into the early hours of the mornings I spent with him, and he never questioned me about the accident or how I was coping. He told me stories of my parents as teenagers growing up, what they were like, as well as their families. It was the only insight I had about who my parents were as individuals. It was fascinating. I had no idea that information would lead to a lot of forgiveness later in life. Richard wanted to know what I thought about the world, music, love, and me. At that time, I felt like every part of me was dead. There was no "me" anymore, only a shell of someone I once was. It was like watching my life play out on a TV screen. With Richard, I felt like I could breathe for the first time in months.

Such friendships, I found, were little glimpses of light, scattered here and there to ease my journey. They seemed insignificant, sometimes just a small spark of hope. I see now that they still supplied some light on my path to help me find my way home.

Vancouver Island became a place of refuge for me, a place to find my head, rejuvenate my spirit and recharge my soul. I continue to visit every couple of years, and Richard always welcomes me with the best hugs and warmest words, that always find their home in my heart.

Then reality abruptly slapped me in the face again. How could I stay any longer? It was over a month now. What kind of person was I to abandon my grief in this beautiful place while my family was suffering at home, still so broken-hearted and sad? I basically had run away. My boyfriend begged me not to return; he said we could start a new life together and get married. He hadn't seen me so happy since before the accident, and was trying to save me from myself. I, however, was desperate to get back to my misery, and my dark penance. A month later, I was back, staring at the four walls of my room, while everything about me slowly unraveled.

My nanny was the world to me. She, in many ways, was my real mother and best friend also. I never saw the woman angry a day in my life. She always told me, "Melanie you're not wrong; the world is!" She knew how excited I was about going to the West Coast and she was thrilled and excited when I said I might stay there to live. When I got home, I surprised her because she had no idea I was ever coming back. I thought I was doing the right thing that my family needed me and I was only breaking their hearts further by staying so far away. To my astonishment and surprise, the first thing she said to me was, "What about Vancouver?" She always cared about my desires and still had dreams for me, even when I couldn't see them. I thought ditching my dreams was the right thing to do for everyone. In that moment, though, she reminded me I needed to do what was right for me. I was nowhere near ready for that. Besides, I was getting good at suffering, after a whole lifetime of practice. I knew how to be sad, angry, and fearful. To be happy, to surrender, or to follow my dreams was unproven territory--unfamiliar and too daunting for me to imagine for myself.

Chapter 3: Breaking Down

Break Down: a breaking down, wearing out, or sudden loss of ability to function efficiently, as of a machine. A loss of mental, physical health or collapse. An analysis, classification of something, division into parts, categories, processes, etc.

A year and a half had passed and it was June 22. To me, it felt as if only five minutes had passed. Everyday was a minefield of potential emotional eruptions. That day, my boyfriend and I had an argument, which wasn't unusual. Our relationship was unhealthy and volatile, even on good days. Everyone has a breaking point and he found his.

He looked at me and said, "Who are you? I don't know who you are anymore. You don't go anywhere; I cook your meals; I wash your clothes; and you barely talk to me. I can't do this anymore." He picked up a bag and began to walk around the room, collecting his things.

I was shocked and then the panic of having someone else leave me set in. He was the only thing I felt I had left. He was my first serious relationship. It had been three years; how could he just walk out? How could he not? I screamed and cried hysterically, even throwing myself to the ground and holding onto his legs as he kicked me off and left. I pleaded and promised things would change, but he was unmoved and slammed the door on my life. I picked up an aluminum camping pot and smashed it onto the floor as hard as I could, denting it in the most awkward ways. I felt like if I stopped, what would I do next? I was alone finally, totally alone. I wanted to die. I kept hitting this pot into the ground until the handle flew off in bits, scattering its shattered pieces across the room. I held my knees tightly into my chest, rocking back and forth for a moment, too afraid to move from that spot.

I knew I had to call someone. There was one person who understood all my secrets and loved me just the same. His name was Mike, and we were best friends. He knew me better than anyone. He was the boy that would have walked through fire for me; but I was totally and selfishly oblivious to his feelings. In an instant, he came to my house, holding me and trying his best to comfort me, and all my fractured pieces. I picked up the phone and called my family doctor. The receptionist put her on the phone immediately, and she asked me if I was thinking about harming myself. I said, "No, but I don't care if anything happens to me."

She suggested that I immediately go to the crisis team at the hospital, where I hadn't set foot since Lana's death. Mike led me in through another entrance to avoid the Emergency department on our way to the third floor. He knew that was more than I could take. I felt like I was dying: my breath was short, my heart was racing, and pounding so hard, I found it difficult to swallow. I kept begging him not to tell anyone where I was. It would kill my poor grandparents. How could I do this to them? I was rushed into a room with a crisis team who spent all of five minutes listening to me, before sending me into a psychiatrist's office.

Something was happening in my mind. I felt like I was in a cloud of confusion. I stuttered and stammered over my words, when suddenly, I was outside my body, watching my sad self falling apart in front of this strange man. I couldn't stop talking; the words just kept spilling out of my mouth. So many words, like it were my last five minutes on the planet, and I had to get them out. If not, I knew I was poisoning myself. I had to eradicate them all from my mind and body.

The psychiatrist got up from his chair and put his hand on my shoulder, saying, "You need a break." Then, once again, like that horrible phone call, telling me Lana was in an accident, my heart and mind went into protection mode. I started to think to myself, *How funny it is for me to have a break? How absurd! And obscene!* I laughed in my mind, thinking, *Oh well, what the hell? I'll probably spend the weekend here. How could this happen to me? It was my job to be strong.* I didn't want anyone to know where I was. I stepped into the hall and asked Mike if he could go to my house and pack me an overnight bag, the angel that he was. He looked shocked and heartbroken, but he left right away.

Two nurses appeared, and one handed me a little, white paper cup. Inside, there were three different colored pills. I was given another paper cup with water to swallow them, and I did. The two nurses escorted me down the hall and we paused for some locked doors to open. Within seconds, their voices became warm, like their words were melting into my ears, and fading into that muffled underwater, off-in-the-distance sound that I heard before in that blinding moment that hurt so bad.

There they were: bouncing, speckled sparrows, hopping on a pavement stone, frantically picking up pieces of dried toast. I don't know how long I was watching them from my window sill, which was wide enough to sit on. The window overlooked a patio space that was enclosed by rounded bars and walls so you couldn't climb, or for some, consider jumping. It was like a giant, grand birdcage for people. The sparrows were funny. They reminded me of my nanny, who loved birds so much. She told me the first word I ever spoke was "bird." I laughed quietly to myself, watching their little bird dances in the sunlight. I thought maybe the stones were too hot for their feet. It was funny and simple and something I hadn't thought in a very long time. I heard my name, and turned my head. Looking over at the nurse, she asked me how I was feeling. An overwhelming rush of heat rose into my face and I felt sick to my stomach and very confused. She asked me if I was okay.

I said, "Did my friend bring my clothes over for me?" She looked puzzled, so I asked, "Is he still here?"

"Melanie, that was over a week ago," she replied.

That was a terrifying moment. I knew I was in the hospital and I knew my name. But although I had just spent over a whole week in this room, it seemed completely strange and unfamiliar to me. I didn't have any recollection of lost time on those days when my soul was so sad, it actually left my body. Had I completely lost my mind? Was this sudden awakening going to reveal what a hollow person I'd become now? Devoid of everything I ever knew or was? I wanted to cry, but nothing happened. There was a very loud numbness that enveloped my head. I couldn't feel sad, happy, or angry; I was only confused, like my ability to feel anything had been removed. The nurse handed me a paper cup with the "crazy candy" in it--pills, pills, and more pills. I was informed that I must attend a group therapy session in one hour. I sat on my bed and waited, trying to figure out what was happening to me.

The nurse came to my door and asked me if I was ready in a tone that told me I didn't have a choice. I walked slowly to the door, feeling weak, dizzy, and as if my feet weren't connected to my body. Leaving the room made me suddenly vulnerable. I was disappointed in myself for being there, for not being able to fix myself, and for losing control.

As I walked down the hallway at the pace of a ninety-year-old woman, I began to take everything in. The smells, the sounds of distant conversations, the doctors passing by, deeply engrossed and fumbling through papers. Were they my papers? At this point, I didn't even know what was wrong with me. Where was everyone? My friends? My family? Why weren't they here? Were they worried or looking for me? I was told later that a lot of them were there; but I have no memory of them. With each room I passed, I looked inside and tried to figure out who surrounded me, and if they were any reflection of what I must look like being in this place. These are "crazy people" and I'm here. I shook my head and thought about being in bed, how I just wanted to lie in it, under the blankets asleep anywhere but here, where I was forced to become consciously aware of this fresh, new hell.

Lunacy: craziness, madness, aberration, absurdity, derangement, distraction, folly, idiocy, imbalance, ineptitude, insanity, mania, psychopathic, psychosis, senselessness, silliness, stupidity.

The first three rooms were empty. It never even dawned on me that the inhabitants of those rooms were actually already at group therapy, but my eyes continued to search for someone like me. I heard giggling as I approached the next doorway. Sitting on the bed were two girls. One was heavier set and wore a hospital gown. Her hair was short and she had a big presence about her. My attention quickly moved to the other girl, who was dressed in plain clothes. At first, I was just drawn to her attractiveness, she was my age and had auburn hair that was smooth and silky looking. It fell softly at her shoulders, and her skin was flawless and looked to be perfectly porcelain. When I caught her smile, I was embarrassed that I was staring. I didn't realize that I had actually stopped in the doorway. They looked at each other, then at me, like they were trying to place me. Then the beautiful girl spoke. She said, "Hi, I'm Jenn; this is Lisa," and even her voice was perfect. It was kind and sweet. She seemed like the kind of girl you could fall in love with in an instant and she was.

I said, "Hey," and half smiled before the nurse gave me a look of, "Let's go." As I turned away, I thought, *why the hell can't I have it all together like that girl? Smart and pretty, working at the hospital... What is wrong with me?* I asked the nurse if there were a lot of volunteers like the girl I had just seen.

The nurse said, "She's not a volunteer, she's a patient." I was shocked, but it was an important discovery for me in learning the many faces of what I thought crazy looked like.

The room was arranged in a circle of chairs, and there were about twenty people of various ages. I was nervous and my mind was foggy. All their faces looked the same to me--a blur. The therapist led the group by having everyone take turns speaking. Some spoke about how they felt, while others shared stories about why they were there. I was the newest member of group, and although I was trying to be polite and listen to all these broken people, I couldn't concentrate on any particular story. I hung my head and tried to remain invisible, dreading my turn and having to share anything in front of all these strangers. But again, reality woke me up and it was my turn, the last in the circle. There were no tears from me as I opened my mouth and desperately tried to hold my composure. I kept my head down, my eyes hidden. I told them how my sister was my best friend, how I felt it was up to me to protect her, and how I failed everyone. The words kept spilling out like a broken levee as though it had happened only five minutes ago. I was so confused, repeating myself and stuttering over my constant apologies to Lana, to the therapist, and to everyone there. When the words finally drained into silence, then sobbing, I looked up at the faces of this circle. I saw the one real thing that was killing me, the look of compassion toward me. Some were wiping their tears with crumpled tissues, and one of the nurses even looked distraught. I cried and cried as they escorted me back to my bed where I stayed for the next whole day.

It was humiliating, baring my soul to complete strangers, and I felt so ashamed. It was like my skin was turned inside out, unprotected and bleeding for everyone to see. The only thing I looked forward to was the paper cup that would take away my constant nausea. You can fool the mind with meds, but you can't fool the heart. Morning came, and I opened my eyes again, only to realize it really had happened and Lana really was dead. Every morning would come like that and my heart exploded with grief daily in my chest.

I was new on the ward and had a lot to learn. There was only a certain amount of time they would let you indulge in any pity party. The next morning, I was ordered to get dressed and fill out my menu for the week. If I refused, they would dress me and pick my meals for me. If I didn't shower, I would be showered. Participation was expected, and not an option. The program was beginning, and a routine needed to be established. Breakfast was brought to our rooms, while lunch and dinner were held in a common room down the hall, and where we were required to dine. In the lunchroom, it smelled like a cafeteria--sterile, steamy, and bland. There were long tables and hard, plastic, multi-colored chairs. There were carts with shelves that had spaces with labels on them. The labels had our names on them. Then I spotted something unusual for a cafeteria. How could anything be unusual in a cafeteria in the psyche ward? It was like it appeared just for me… a piano. Music was the tiny bit of sanity that had carried me this far. Even as a child, my parents fought so much, I would often leave early for school, just to escape. I would attend mass and sing the hymns. The music was my salvation. It was the first thing that recaptured my interest and gave me hope, One little thing to look forward to in a place that made no sense, not the hospital, but my head.

Chapter 4: Unlikely Friends

Therapy: the treatment of physical, mental, or social disorders or disease.

The first time I walked into the cafeteria for lunch, I stood there, filled with anxiety, fighting desperately not to have a meltdown over leaving my room. It's hard to explain the irrationality of anxiety disorders or panic attacks. The simplest tasks, like feeding yourself, or finding a seat, when cast in a public situation where you're spotlighted, can be crippling. In my mind, I knew those were simple things and probably nobody had even noticed me, but I felt like I somehow had egg on my face. The room became very big and very small at the same time, and my heart raced. I wanted to leave, even though I could see my name clearly labeled on the lunch cart. *Just walk over and pick up the damn food!* My mind kept telling me it was no big deal; then betrayed me in the next thought by saying, *Look at you! Just look at you! Who do you think you are showing your face here? Then where will I sit? Alone? Looking pathetic? Or intrude on a fuller table? Which colored chair should I choose? Which number out of the six chairs? Do I sit near the window to look outside? Or sit near the door so I can escape?* The whole process of getting the food into my body became just another unhappy ordeal.

The two girls whom I met earlier saw me. We made eye contact and they invited me to join them. Lisa jumped right out of her chair, grabbing my tray from the cart as I reached for it. As if she could sense my inner struggle, she placed it on the table. So there it was on the table--my lunch and my inner struggle... How did this strange girl even know my name? Everyone began to pick apart the food trays. Discussions about "What was half decent?" "What was horrible?" and "How to get extra things like chocolate milk instead of plain white" popped up. Someone asked, "So why are you here?"

Before I could answer, Lisa piped up and said, "She's got Post Traumatic Stress Disorder and her shrink thinks she's Manic Depressive." I looked puzzled and stunned, but she smiled and told me she overheard the psychiatrist and nurse talking in my room a few weeks ago. All conversations bled out into the quiet vacuum of my head. What was this information? Manic what? Post traumatic-what-the-hell? Whatever was messed up about me, now I was being accepted into this group of unlikely friends, and I felt like I just joined my very own Breakfast Club, a group of misfits, rejects, but much more than that. They knew things that no one else could fathom. I imagine it's like people who go through war together. It's an experience so fragile, but horrible that it creates a bond between them. It's hard for others to understand if they haven't shared such critical experiences. The sad thing was, if we bumped into each other on the street, I don't think we would have ever spoken to one another.

I try and think about those kinds of judgmental avoidances when I meet people today. Everyone has a unique story that deserves to be heard, and everyone deserves to find friends wherever they go. We were the most unlikely friends. I was introduced to a few others before meeting Alistair. He was the only guy on our floor, a little older than I, mildly handsome, depressed, and interesting as hell. He chain-smoked and kept interesting treasures in his room. Alistair was a charming, neurotic alcoholic like my father. There were many different people I met in those few months, but no one made the lifelong impressions on me that Lisa, Jenn and Alistair did. They couldn't have been any other three humans. They were like the piano, there in that cafeteria, somehow waiting just for me.

After lunch, one-by-one, everyone exited until I was left alone in that big room, staring at that old, black piano. My anxiety prevented me from going over to it, just in case someone saw me. I was frightened to do or say anything that was in any way happy. It was a delicate tightrope walk. I didn't want to offend anyone with the sound of the piano, but I also didn't want someone to think that since I could play, now I was okay. I wasn't ready to be okay with anything.

I was still reeling from the diagnosis I heard about myself. It was one thing to have PTSD as a result of such an awful thing happening, but to be diagnosed as also having Manic Depressive disorder? This was not a thing that could happen to me, it was part of who I was, as well as what I was becoming. How could things possibly get worse? I thought my life sucked before, and now I was crazy too. I thought this therapy crap was supposed to make people feel better? No one told me that I'd feel a lot worse before I felt better. I had this new information, which scared me and I started to get very angry.

I demanded to see the psychiatrist, and he took me into his office right away. I told him what I heard and insisted on his explanation of what was happening to me. Suddenly, I felt like I needed to justify myself, to rationalize their diagnoses, and prove that I was just there because my little sister died. But at that moment, just as those words left my mouth, I knew there was more going on. It was an overwhelming revelation. I just happened to have endured a devastating event that presented the opportunity for me to discover that I also had a lifelong struggle with depression. I always believed it was because of other people's nonsense. My mother had three bad marriages and became fanatically religious. My father wasn't any better with a history of failed relationships along with addictions to alcohol and drugs. My childhood was chaotic. But it was all I knew. I thought being depressed was just part of life. You're sad most of the time, waiting for those few happy moments. It's heartbreaking to think that I felt that way as early as age seven. I broke down and started talking about everything that ever happened to me from my earliest memory. I couldn't stop unloading. I didn't feel better. It was like someone kicked the snot out of me every time I left a therapy session. Everything hurt in my body, my mind, and my soul. Afterwards, I wouldn't talk. I'd cry and sleep and sleep. Every time I went into that office, however, it kept coming out of my mouth like I was possessed and incurable.

Then, there were my new friends who had taken me into their circle of trust. It was a sanctuary where I got glimpses of love and hope in the darkest of places, but it also showed me sides of people that were almost never seen by others. The most raw view of a human being is when he or she suffers. We all revealed the ugliest parts of our pain to each other. I made some of the deepest connections I ever had with myself and other human beings. It was sharing the same place, without having to say the right things or do anything special. It's what I learned about myself from their presence that was the most precious gift I found.

I wasn't the only one! That's one of the first steps to finding inner peace, when you realize you are not the only one who is suffering. I started to recognize the looks on their faces, anyone who came back from a therapy session of some sort. They appeared to be emotionless zombies at first glance--drained, washed out, wandering down the halls back to their rooms. We always went back to our rooms. They were both our safe havens and our private torture chambers. But I sensed there was something else in all of those emotionally beaten faces. They were dormant volcanoes, just waiting.

Some people were quite forthcoming and shared immediately what happened to get them committed. Alistair was an addict. Jenn was clinically depressed. She had a great family, lots of friends, but a serious chemical imbalance. I had endured a major trauma. We all shared our rooms. I had the room to myself for the first few weeks, and then a middle-aged woman moved in, named Mary. She was so nice and had a very maternal personality. The first few nights she was there, we stayed up really late, whispering in the dark as long as we could before the sleeping pills kicked in. I told her my story.

When I told her about the heavy snow the day of the funeral, and how it clung to every branch so delicately and perfectly, she got up from her bed and rummaged through her things. She brought over a photograph to me. She said, "Did it look like this?" I was amazed. The photo looked exactly like the day of Lana's funeral, as if it had been taken that very day. She said she wanted me to have it. The next morning, they took her for some kind of shock therapy, or so she told me. Whether or not this was true, I don't know; except she was never the same after whatever treatment she received. She didn't talk anymore, just stayed in her bed; and oddly, the nurses left her alone most days. I would pull her blankets over her shoulders if I noticed they had fallen, but there were no more late night talks. One day, I returned to the room after lunch, and she was gone, all her things packed up and gone. The room was all mine again.

There was one other person who didn't share a room, Lisa. After dinner one night, Jenn, Lisa and I went back to her room. The nurse looked at me and said, "Nothing sharp?" After looking me up and down, she let me pass into Lisa's room. Lisa didn't even bat an eye at the nurse. She seemed always pleasant and in a good mood. Appearances, however, were deceiving. I sat on the bed, and she wanted to give me a CD she thought I would like. It was "Lisa Loeb nine tails" and the only music we had. We played that CD a billion times and it became a crazy soundtrack to our disheveled lives. As she handed it to me, the sleeve of her housecoat slightly moved past her wrist. I was embarrassed and shocked. Those weren't a few scars from a botched suicide attempt. There were scars on top of the scars, dozens of cuts across her wrists, all the way up her arms. Then I looked down, so she wouldn't notice that I saw her self–mutilation. Every bit of uncovered flesh was covered in a mess of lacerations, cuts, marks everywhere on her body. She was known as a "cutter."

The sleeping pills we were given were very powerful and left the most awful taste in your mouth the next morning. So when I say that her screams were so loud, it woke me from a drug-induced sleep, you better believe they were loud and violent. I had never heard anyone scream like that. It was a voice filled with pure terror. I could hear the nurses and orderlies being paged. There was loud crash as well as a struggle that spilled into the hallway as they dragged her down the hall to the "Time Out" room. I sat there, freaked out, wondering what could possibly make someone so upset. I admit to breaking down and being hysterical at times, but this was altogether different. This was a person immersed in total fear, in a way I've never experienced. It was like the boogie man jumped out of her closet.

Later, I learned the monster in her closet was her own father, who allowed his drunken friends to rape her ruthlessly for years while she was just a child. Her father also beat her every day until she was removed from the house at age sixteen. She had given birth to three children as a result of the abuse and they were all taken from her. I also found out Lisa was committed to a long term-facility and treatment. As sad as it sounds, at least I knew one day, I'd get out. Realizing that, at that moment, my life didn't seem as bad as hers. That night, I crept into the hall, unsure of what I would see. We weren't allowed to leave our rooms at night. I knew that everyone was busy with the current situation, and I could get out of bed without grief from the night nurse. We were checked on every few hours during the night. These were little reminders that we weren't in a hotel or spa on vacation; it was a suicide watch, and this was a hospital psychiatric ward. As I peeked out of my doorway, I saw Jenn doing the same. We looked at each other, and without a word, our eyes shared a tacit secret. We already knew to keep it between us; we had seen and heard the most raw, most vulnerable side of another human being. It was ugly and painful to watch, but we felt privileged to have witnessed this great suffering. We both knew it would never leave us, and we had a choice to use this information to empower us or break us down. I hurried back to my bed, pulling the blankets over my head, and lay still in the darkness for hours.

The floor was quiet the next day, so I ventured out to the birdcage, where Alistair and I smoked cigarettes and talked about his travels around the world. He seemed to have a few more privileges than we. He had day passes. He could have a friend or family member come visit and sign him out for a few hours. Every time he came back, he brought something to show us. I told him that I loved Tolkien and Alistair came into my room one day with an old book of rare Tolkien drawings. He said he bought it in an antique shop in England. It was leather bound, and had white, translucent paper that divided every page. It was incredible. He was nervous about leaving it with me. I begged him to, so I could copy some of the pictures into my sketchbook. I remember how bright the sun was splashing through my windows as I dumped a box of pencil crayons over the bed, trying to find the exact colors to replicate the sketches. I was a perfectionist in my artwork and everything that fueled me creatively. My favorite sketch was of a bird. I thought one day it might make a great tattoo, a tattoo for the outside. Inside, I had enough permanent marks.

One day, while returning from a therapy session, I was bombarded in the hallway by Jenn and Lisa. They were giddy and excited as they dragged me to the nurses' station. Jenn pulled out a box of hair dye and asked if we could dye her hair. The nurse said yes, so we piled into the public shower/bathroom and closed the door. We laughed and joked about her hair falling out, or possibly turning orange. We were like normal teenage girls at a slumber party. The three of us were having a good time, doing something normal. The volume got so loud, a nurse opened the door, which surprised us so much, Jenn fell into the tub. We laughed until we cried, it was so funny. It had been so very long since I could genuinely smile or laugh, but I was okay. There was no one there judging me; these girls had seen me at the lowest point in my life and still liked me. The greatest gift you can give someone is your full attention unconditionally. I didn't have to think about the future, and I had no past with these girls. We were all very present in the bathroom, letting go of our pains for a few minutes of pure joy.

Chapter 5: Heart & Soul

It was one of my most cherished memories--Canada Day, July 1st and there we were: Jenn, Lisa, Alistair and I, sitting in the birdcage, waiting for darkness to fall. We had special permission to stay outside extra late to watch the fireworks, not all of them, but for a little while. The view from the birdcage was beautiful. It overlooked a large part of the city, so we could catch fireworks from all over. We sat side-by-side against the cement wall and passed a pot joint between us, which Alistair managed to smuggle in that day. We were all so connected and happy that evening. Jenn suggested that we make it a tradition after we got out, to meet every Canada Day and watch the fireworks. We all enthusiastically agreed. It never happened; it was a different world on the outside. Some things had to stay behind, I guess, to lighten the load in order to move forward. The floor was quiet that night and I let the sleeping pill take me without a fight.

Routine: a customary or regular course of procedure commonplace tasks, chores, or duties as must be done regularly or at specified intervals; typical or everyday activity.

I was becoming a regular observer of all the routines around me. The hospital staff had a routine as well as the patients, us. As individuals, we all had our own routines and maybe a little OCD too. Every day in the lunchroom, I would wait until almost everyone left. If there were not too many people, I'd wander over to the piano and just look at it… longingly; but I still had no courage to actually sit on the bench. My fingers were frozen by my sides. Then I would drag my feet into my slippers, and go out onto the patio for a smoke. This went on for weeks. Eventually, I wasn't going to the cafeteria for the food, and I lost thirty pounds while I was in there. I couldn't get that image out of my head: the black upright piano, waiting for me.

One day, I had a visitor join me for lunch--Sonya. I was so happy to see a familiar face, especially hers. She had no expectations and just accepted me as I was. At the time, she was living with her boyfriend and a roommate, and she said money was tight. I offered her my lunch and she scarfed it down like she had never eaten food before.

Then she said, "Mmmmm, it was *so* good…" Good? I almost thought *she* needed to be committed at this point. Then it got even funnier. We realized that some people were out on their day passes, so their lunches would just be thrown out. Sonya ate three meals that day in one sitting! I tease her about it to this day. After lunch, she said, "Ah look! They've got a piano in here! You must love that," as she walked over to it. I had a choice to make at that moment. *Do I let her know how messed up I really am? And tell her about the panic attacks I have over this piano on a daily basis? Or do I put on a good front that I'm doing a lot better, and play something?* I walked over to join her like it was no big deal, and pulling out the bench, I sat on it. The keys looked a million miles wide, and my hands felt so small; the room was still and no one made a sound. I brought my two hands up to the pretty white keys and began to play John Lennon's "Imagine." From that moment on, I spent every day tinkering away on those keys after lunch. It was before group, so it worked out perfectly for me; after group there was nothing left

At times, people would enter and exit the cafeteria; some would listen for a few minutes, but no one would stick around. One day, I noticed a new face. She was East Indian and very young, probably fifteen. She was quiet and always came in later, sitting alone at the table. I never saw or heard her speak when we passed each other in the hall. She never spoke at group either. One day, however, as I sat at the piano, trying to figure out a song I'd written, I sensed I was being watched. There she was, standing beside me at the bench. She asked me if I could teach her to play something, and I said sure. I scooted my butt over so we could share the bench. I began to show her the melody to "Heart & Soul." She was so excited and soon looked forward to our daily lesson. It took a couple of days, but she figured out her part. We just smiled and laughed whenever we made a mistake, but we persisted with the lesson and she learned something new. Then one day, while we sat there at the big black piano, she told me her father raped her and burst into tears, collapsing into my chest. I felt like a big sister for the first time in a long time. The nurses came to the rescue with crazy candy for both of us. The next day, the girl was gone. I never saw her again, but I've never forgotten her.

I continued to make progress in therapy. By progress, I mean, I could get out of bed and do what I was told. It still hurt me to breathe whenever I thought about Lana. There were good and bad days, and I began to realize that everyday was the best or worst day of someone's life, somewhere. It felt like we all took turns. When I was first admitted to the hospital, for the first few weeks, I didn't want any contact with the outside world. I just wanted to hide. I was embarrassed for people I knew to see me like this; and I still felt so much pressure to keep things together for everyone else. I just wanted to be left alone. I found solace in the isolation of the hospital and its routines. Leaving its sheltering comfort seemed like a far-off dream, and not a pleasant one. I felt like there was nothing left for me on the outside, nothing to look forward to. All the joy had vanished from everything I once found pleasure in. I never felt so empty in my life.

Epiphany: a sudden, intuitive perception of or insight into the reality or essential meaning of something, usually initiated by some simple, homely, or commonplace occurrence or experience.

Having just had a shower, I was barely dressed, wearing only a towel wrapped around me. I bundled up my dirty clothes in my arms and reached for the doorknob. It opened and I dropped half of what I was carrying onto the floor. When I looked up, I realized I wasn't alone in my room. There, sitting in my window sill, just as I was a month earlier, was Ben! He pretended not to notice me; he was kind of a joker that way. Ben was my high school sweetheart and also Sonya's roommate at the time. He was one of the few people who knew what was going on. He smiled and said, "Get dressed. I'm taking you out of here," as if he were breaking me out in some kind of Bonnie and Clyde adventure. I thought to myself, *Oh no! He has no idea how messed up I really am.* I was terrified at that moment. It's funny, though, how the right person at the right time can give you wings.

Ben was charming, artistic, intelligent and handsome; but he could be dark, moody and self-absorbed as well. He was the first boy I think I really fell in love with. I was sixteen when we dated; it was very innocent and sweet. Ben was the quintessential high school sweetheart. He could make me lose my breath and forget all my words with just a glance. Here he was, beautiful as ever, standing in the middle of the hurricane that I'd become. I was such a mess inside, but I put on a good face and left the room. We were given times and instructions for my day pass. He looked at me reassuringly and held my hand all the way back to his place. The familiar buildings and streets where I grew up all seemed out of place and new to me. Even the sun felt different on my skin than it did inside the safety of the hospital birdcage. My mind and heart started to race and I was suddenly in doubt that I had done the right thing. It was a tough fight for me not to panic and have him see me fall apart right there on the sidewalk. I just concentrated on his hand holding mine, and his eyes reassuring me that he would take care of me that day. To this day, I don't think he realized how petrified I was. To him, he was a good friend doing a favour for another friend. To me, however, it was so much more.

We arrived at the house and no one was home that afternoon. We went to his room and he made me soup. It sounds so simple, but it was the best bowl of soul soup I ever had. We talked about what it was like to be in the hospital. He told me how he also thought about going there, due to his struggle with depression. It was probably the most honest conversation we ever had. We talked for hours about our lives and our demons. I saw him in a brand new light. Ben was just one more person out there, challenged with the conflicts of life and trying to find some peace inside his head. I didn't feel so alone. Then he smiled and asked me if I wanted to see his new pillow. I naively walked over to his bed, where he instantly tackled me, kissing me passionately. I felt alive again. For the first time I could remember, there really *was* a life outside of the hospital waiting for me. Ben had unknowingly proven to me that I was still likable, attractive and hadn't used up all my chances for a good life. That was the gift Ben gave me, and one that I'll never forget.

After returning to my room at the hospital, I thought about our afternoon and felt a little braver about what was on the other side, the *outside.* Since I did so well that week, I was allowed to leave for a few hours on my own. My bravery was short-lived when something unexpected happened. On my way back to the hospital, on one sunny afternoon after taking a walk, I fell apart. I came to the traffic light on Simcoe Street and looked across the road at the other side, waiting for the light to change. The traffic was heavy and moving fast. Suddenly, I imagined seeing my sister standing on the other side of the street. I thought to myself, *If I just step onto the road, it will all stop*. The noise in my head, the panic attacks, and the searing chest pains that plagued me incessantly. *It would all stop*. Then as quickly as the thought came, the light changed and the cars stopped. The tears started streaming down my face, and I began to run as fast as I could back to the hospital. I somehow ended up running right into the Emergency ward. I had been trying to avoid that place at all costs. The place where this whole mess all started, and now, here I was, standing there, confused and overwhelmed. I fell to the ground and cried and rocked myself into a shivering ball. A nurse spotted my hospital bracelet and brought me back to my floor, like a lost child that wandered off. I immediately went into the psychiatrist's office and told him what happened. I never went out alone again for the rest of my stay.

I had a meeting with my doctors about a week later. I sat at a long table with several doctors to discuss my possible release. It's not that I didn't think I would ever leave, but the reality of my release suddenly terrified me. I didn't know how to cope. I felt like I had nothing to go back to. I wasn't close to my parents. Most of my friends were busy, living their lives and building their careers, doing what normal people did. They were all sympathetic, but I didn't feel like I belonged anywhere or to anyone.

I felt that hot, sick feeling in my mouth suddenly as the panic rose inside of me. I protested, "I can't leave! I don't know what to do out there!" It sounded so stupid coming out of my mouth, but I really didn't know how to function properly. The thought of even making my own meals seemed like an impossible, overwhelming task. To go to the grocery store, to perform a normal routine and fill my time made me want to cry, and I did. At the same time, I was utterly exhausted by so many tears. How the hell did I have any tears left? I was mad at myself for still being able to cry at all. My eyes just saw what they wanted, while my mind raced to terrible places on its own. My body was wasting away because I couldn't feel hunger.

I needed to figure out how to regain some control. Nothing belonged to me anymore, it seemed, except my suffering. I had bottomed out. I started to question everything I ever knew. What did I believe in? Did I have faith in anything? Not just in God, but life and the whole universe? I was so empty. *Could anything fill this void?* The doctors assured me it was okay to feel that way. They said they weren't releasing me at that moment. We were just talking about my progress and the future possibilities for when I *would* leave the hospital. It was exactly what I needed to hear. Now I could begin preparing myself to start my life over. Every minute of your life is a chance for you to start over.

There was something that really began to speak to me while I was there. Every night before bed, we had a guided meditation. We brought our blankets and lay on the floor, listening to a relaxation CD. Some nights, it would be: picture yourself on a beach; the breeze is blowing… Other nights, it was about learning to breathe deeply. Despite my mind's wandering and busy wheel-spinning, afterwards, I always felt a sense of peace, even if only for a little while. I began to look forward to these meditations. After leaving the hospital, I continued to listen to meditation CDs for ten years. It was the only way I could fall asleep! If that sounds like things never got better for me, they did. Depression is a lifelong struggle, and losing someone precious never goes away. Our perceptions of these things change, however, and grow when we do. If we don't move beyond or try to change, we risk becoming imprisoned in those dark places forever. We will never learn our true purpose for this wonderful life. Meditation was another tool, which I was graciously given, and still lovingly use to this day.

Chapter 6: Visitors

Visitor: a person who visits, as for reasons of friendship, business, duty, travel, or the like.

I will never forget those friends who came to visit me at the hospital. I hope they all know how grateful I was and what it meant to my recovery and to me. The food was terrible, except to Sonya, of course. But Joanne felt for me. She made me homemade spaghetti and smuggled it in. I was so high on meds, I thanked her for it three days later, thinking I had just eaten it. We still laugh about it. Then there were the thousands of card games with Mike. We always played Crazy Eights because I thought that was funny. What else should you play in the psyche ward, but *CRAZY* Eights? He usually lost, which made it even funnier. I teased him for losing to me, "the crazy girl," and his face would turn red, while his smile just tore me to pieces. These little moments of laughter started filling in the empty spaces of my life.

I think one of the best times I had was with my little toy poodle, named Rufus. My friend, Andre, was taking care of him for me while I was at the hospital. One day, he came to visit and entered my room, wearing a large jacket, which was odd because it was August. When he opened his jacket, there was my little dog, Rufus, with him to visit me. Rufus jumped all over the beds, he was so happy to see me. He cried and jumped from bed to bed, whimpering, and I was afraid he might pee. I was so happy to see him, I was in shock. We laughed and scurried around the room, trying to keep him from barking. We never did get caught, but I often wondered if the nurses let things slide sometimes, knowing that these little indulgences meant all the difference to the patients' healing.

My parents never came to visit, but one of my father's friends, Pete, came after he heard. He brought me a bag filled with scratch tickets and girly magazines. He didn't stay long, but he messed up my hair and patted me on the head, saying, "Take it easy, kiddo," and left. It was perfect. It was short and sweet; no questions or expectations.

Just when I thought things were looking up, the sky fell on me again. There was something that I hadn't really dealt with at the time, and that was my break-up. He never called or visited, but his sister did. I remember sitting on the bed, having a nice, lengthy conversation with her about everything, *but* her brother. Then, out of nowhere, she said he had a new girlfriend, whom everyone was saying looked just like me. I couldn't believe it! Here I was in the hospital, losing my mind, and after three years, it took him all of a few weeks to move on! I was devastated. I lost it. I began screaming at her, "How could you come here and tell me this? Like it's no big deal?!" I screamed at her, "Get out!" over and over until she did.

I went into the bathroom, locked the door, and bawled my eyes out on the cold floor. How could he do this? It wasn't even about him, really. It was just another reminder of my losses, of no one waiting for me out there. I was so hurt. Something we were never allowed to do in the hospital was to lock a door. It was a big no-no. Within minutes, two orderlies were in the bathroom, telling me I needed to calm down. I was hysterical, kicking and hollering. Then they physically dragged me out, gave me a shot of something, and I was put into the "Time Out" room. Within seconds, I was defenseless and out of my mind--unable to talk, walk or think clearly. When I felt the meds hitting me, I began to laugh out loud. I was pissed off for not being allowed to feel anything, even though it was my own fault. I thought it was funny that I actually thought I was getting better. As I laughed, I must have truly looked like a madwoman.

The days passed and I was feeling distant and quiet. I walked down the hall, looking for some company and happened to glance into Lisa's room. It was empty. Everything was gone, as if she were never there. I ran down the hall to Jenn's room, where I found her looking at some trinkets she had. She loved frogs, and they will always remind me of her. I asked her where Lisa was, and she said that she had been transferred. I left, feeling sad and sorry that I never got to say goodbye. I went out alone to the birdcage to have a smoke, where Mike found me. He had a surprise for me; he brought my guitar. At that point, Alistair and Jenn came out, and I sat in the sunshine, clumsily playing a few Joni Mitchell songs. They were surprised at the voice that came out; I was surprised that I could still sing. It wasn't just the dancing sparrows who sang anymore.

Next to go was Alistair. Again, no goodbyes, just an empty room, waiting for the next patient. So much had happened in those rooms. Life was moving forward quickly and it took my breath away. The fact that life kept moving was hard for me to accept. As they were released, one-by-one, into the real world, I knew my turn was coming. It felt like we had lived a whole lifetime in just those few months. I knew I was not the same person I was when I came in. I had no idea who I was anymore, or what awaited me in my real world. Jenn and I were released at the end of August, but I only saw her outside of the hospital twice that year. We never spoke again.

Upon my release, I entered an outpatient program called "Interact," which I attended for six months. It consisted of daily group therapy sessions. We even had a pharmacologist come in and explain what our medications were and what they did. I found it fascinating to know what these crazy candy drugs did. Later on, I used that knowledge to abuse my medication. The road to freedom was not smooth. I was out of the hospital, but still not ready to face life fully, or cleanly. It still surprises me that despite all the therapy I had, no one warned me how scary it would be on the outside. Not to mention suddenly having the responsibility for taking serious medication. Throughout my stay, I had many medication and dosage changes. The doctors play with your head until they find the right combination of drugs that work. Once you leave, usually they slowly wean you off most of the drugs. The antidepressants are usually the only ones that you keep taking. Trying to face the world after you've been given something that numbs all those feelings you should be dealing with is pretty terrifying to just quit. Reassessment didn't happen as often as I thought it should. The Interact program was a new group of people with a whole new set of problems and issues. I felt like I was wearing my trauma like a badge of hardcore hospital honor. I had just come from the loony bin and these people were depressed because they lost their jobs? Or their boyfriends left. I felt annoyed at these people and their so-called pain. They had no clue of the people I had just spent the past few months with, who really had problems.

It seemed obvious to me, as they spoke every day, what was wrong with their lives and how easily they could fix them. It was terribly arrogant and insensitive of me to think that way. I was still angry and hurt, trying to work through my own issues. When I told my story, no one gave me any advice. At first, they said nothing, looking kind of lost for words. I thought to myself, *That's right. What are you all going to say to me?* Eventually, they did start giving me advice, and to my amazement, it was good, kind and genuine. I felt sorry that I pre-judged them. I was so tired of learning lessons; I just wanted to get better. I was so impatient. As the weeks and months passed, I found myself giving the group advice and trying to help more often and be as encouraging as possible. I felt good when I made others feel better. Then it dawned on me: *why I am still here?* I found myself spending every session talking to everyone else about fixing their lives. I needed to start fixing mine, so I quit.

This is not where I have an "Aha!" moment and actually fix my life. Instead, I threw the world's biggest pity party. I quickly found that alcohol and street drugs turned my legal meds into a whole new event. I went to the bar three nights a week, and poor Mike would drag me home to put me to bed. I would wake up in the morning or afternoon, with no clue where I was or how I got home. But no one could tell me otherwise. I didn't want to hear it. I felt like I had just been through hell, so give me a break. I lied to my GP, saying I lost my pills, and a million other excuses. She would give me new prescriptions and why not? She had known me my whole life. For appearances sake, I seemed like an honest girl who had lost her little sister in a terrible accident, and was still having a rough time. Not a druggie on a self-destruct mission, now with a serious addiction.

There were three moments that changed everything about my drug problem. The first was when I was at a party and took a handful of pills. I said to myself, *I wonder if I'll wake up*. Then I thought, *Oh well, it's too late now*, and I passed out. Yes, I woke up, and remembered clearly what I had done, with regret and shame. There was a little voice inside me that said, "Do you really have a good enough excuse for messing your life up?" I was young, healthy, attractive and smart. In that same voice, there was a little cryptic admonishment that kept hinting I could somehow do better than I gave myself credit for. I think I was more afraid of success than failure.

The second event was a night when I was so messed up, I went to a friend's house in the middle of the night, absolutely wasted. I don't know how I even got there. Her husband took one look at me and physically dragged me into the bathroom. He forced me down on the ground, in front of the toilet, and told me we weren't leaving until I made myself puke. He then emptied my pockets and flushed all my pills down the toilet in front of me. I cried and cried watching them go down.

I just remember him screaming at me, "What the f--k are you doing to yourself?"

The third event was the game changer. My ex finally showed up on my doorstep. I was alone and invited him in. He apologized for not being there for me. It was really emotional, and we slept together. I told him that if we were not going to be together, I couldn't just sleep with him. It hurt too much after everything else. I told him it was over and he left. It was so hard, but I needed to move on. I spent the next eight weeks partying hard. I was tired all the time. I assumed it was because I was hung over. One night, on the way to the bar, I took a pregnancy test. It was positive. I had every right to mess up my own life, but not the life of this baby. People could say what they wanted about me, but I was not going to be called a bad mom. I quit everything cold turkey. It was hard, and I was pretty sick coming off the meds. I immediately devoted my life to this baby. I read every book I could find about babies and parenting. There was no turning back.

Chapter 7: Growing

Grow: to increase by natural development, as any living organism. To form and increase in size. To arise or issue as a natural development from an original happening, circumstance. To become greater or larger.

I attended prenatal classes with my girlfriends. One day, Sonya said she was the dad during introductions and everyone burst into laughter. It eased the sting of being a single mom for a second. My ex told me he wasn't ready for a baby and I was crazy to think I could do it by myself. Call me crazy, will you? That just made my decision clearer and fortified my determination to prove to everyone I *could* do this. I would do it alone and show everyone, especially myself.

The pregnancy was a time of deep reflection for me. It was lonely, and I was scared most days. I walked a mile a day. I didn't even drink tea or coffee. I ate healthy and had a non-eventful pregnancy. Physically, I felt like a million dollars. I gave birth to a healthy baby girl, and she was perfect. I discovered quickly who my real friends were, and I surrounded myself with them. I began to mend my relationships with my family. My mother was thrilled to be a grandmother, and I thought that although our relationship wasn't perfect, maybe this was a chance for all of us to start over. She became the best grandmother, so great, I often wondered why she was never like that with me. Maybe she just needed a chance to start over as well.

This baby brought so much joy to everyone. It was she and I against the world. I wanted her to have all the things I never did as a child: peace, stability, confidence, and to live fearlessly as all children should. Her biological father came back for a couple of months. He wasn't ready to settle down and be a good father, and I wouldn't compromise. I filed for sole custody. He stood in front of the justice of the peace and told her what an amazing mom I was, that he was completely irresponsible, and in no position to be a good role model, much less a father, and signed the papers. It wasn't easy to stand there and watch him walk away, not so much from me, but the most wonderful child. *How could he not be as madly in love with her as I was?* And want to change, like I did? But deep down, I knew why. He suffered with depression too. He never felt like he was good enough. A few years later, he admitted to me in a random phone call that he felt like he needed to let us go, just so we could have a good life. That made me so sad. When we met, I was seventeen and we had everything negative in common. We hated the world, we came from broken families, and we thought we understood each other's pain. In the end, I just wanted more, I wanted to be happy. But when I was happy, it seemed to plunge him further into darkness. I don't know how we lasted as long as we did.

I grew a lot while he was gone, and didn't even realize it until one day.

He said to me, "When your friends come into the room, you light up, but when I come into the room, you just tolerate me." I was shocked and denied it, but he was right,

I didn't need him anymore, and I was no longer in love with him. He came for a few visits and we didn't see him again. A few years later, I received a phone call from his mother at six-thirty in the morning, saying he had taken his own life. It broke my heart. I was in that dark place once, but I was fortunate enough to find help. It took me a long time to heal and eventually forgive him. I was so angry that he never left us any chance or choice in the matter. Now, with the realization that those moments were never mine, along with understanding my own pain, I can appreciate the times we shared together, both good and bad, and forgive him.

In the meantime, my white knight rides in a Volkswagen. I remember sitting on my couch with my friend, Geordie. I was bawling my eyes out on his shoulder, whining how I was never going to meet anyone. I was twenty-one with a kid and a ton of baggage; who would want me? Who would be mature enough for all of that? I thought it was hopeless. I was lonely and a single mom, but I couldn't just settle for anyone. This was a package deal. I wanted someone looking for the real thing. At the same time, I was terrified to let anyone in. A few weeks later, Geordie called and said, "I'm coming over to jam. Would you mind if I brought a friend?" I thought it odd because he always brought a friend or entourage; why the courtesy call on this day? When they arrived, I was introduced to his friend, Jeff, whom I asked if he played guitar. He burst out laughing, and then I said, "Oh, do you sing?" to which he laughed even more. Then the light bulb went off: I was being set up. After they left, Geordie called me and asked if I would ever go on a date with that guy? Then he called Jeff and asked him if he'd ever go on a date with me? And the answer from both parties was yes, but that wasn't the whole story.

I only share that little event with you because it's a reminder that you never know when life-changing opportunities will arise; or when the universe or God tries to reveal something to you. You never know when things may take that karmic loop and come back around to find you. There are no accidents in life.

After Lana died, my boyfriend and father tried to convince me to get my driver's license. I jokingly said I didn't want to be seen in the Junkers they were driving. They said, "If we buy you the car you want, will you do it?"

I laughed and said, "I want a VW Bug." So we bought one! Of course, like everything else, the promises to fix it up were quickly forgotten and it sat parked in the yard for months. I often sat in the car by myself and read, just to get away from everyone.

One day, I came home and my boyfriend said, "Oh yeah, by the way, I sold your car. The guy's coming over tonight to get it." I went through the roof. We had a huge fight until there was a knock at the door. I marched up the stairs--stomp! stomp! stomp! and winged the door open to the poor guy standing there, totally clueless as to what my problem was.

I called out, "He's here!" and stormed back down the stairs. Then a funny thought occurred to me: *that guy was really cute!* I watched out the window as my little bug was towed away. I asked my boyfriend, "What was his name? Maybe when he fixes up the car, he could take me for a ride?" He laughed and said, "They call him Hoy." I thought, *Great! A nickname! What are the odds I'll ever see him again?*

Years passed and the first few weeks that Jeff and I dated, he began to introduce me to his friends. One in particular seemed familiar to me, but I couldn't place him. One night, I said to Jeff, "I think your friend used to work with my ex at a welding factory."

To my surprise, Jeff said, "Hey, I know who your ex is; he sold me my first Bug."

I said, "Your nickname is Hoy?" he smiled and told me that after he left my house that day, he and his brother-in-law joked, saying he should have bought the girl with the car. So my knight in shining VW armor was always there, waiting for our paths to cross.

The things we want sometimes are never as far away as they seem. I could never have imagined, in that brief moment, the stranger at the front door would be my future husband, best friend, and the most amazing father to our children I could ask for.

Chapter 8: Forgiveness

Forgiveness: To grant pardon for or remission of (an offense, debt, etc.); absolve. To give up all claim on account. To cease to feel resentment against: to forgive one's enemies.

I once heard that to forgive someone means not to hold someone else responsible for how you feel.

The things we want sometimes are never as far away as they seem. I must also say the things we hide from are never as far away as they seem either. There was some unfinished business I had with the boy from the accident. He was still there in the back of my mind, a sore spot in my psyche. I still feared running into him somewhere, even these many years after the accident. I would put it at the back of my mind, and try to forget about him, but he was always there. I learned to let go of things that didn't serve me, and tried to understand how to be a compassionate person in this life. I was about to put it to the test.

A few years ago, I received a friend request from a girl I knew in high school on a very popular social networking site. I accepted it with hesitance, because although I knew of her, we never hung around together or were really friends in school. I thought maybe she was interested in my music. Being a singer/songwriter, I get a lot of requests from other musicians and fans, so it's not that odd. Except this girl was never into music from what I could remember. So I decided to search through her friends' list to see whom she knew. There was his name--as plain as day—Tim, the boy from the accident, right there in front of me. I felt sick at first, wondering if they hung out together and creeped my profile? I suddenly realized that he had access to my life, my photos, and he was right there, even after all these years. Surprisingly, I also realized I had access to his profile, I had a way to contact him, I knew where to find him. Now this discovery grew much scarier.

What do I do? Was it a coincidence that this girl contacted me and they were friends? The more I thought about it, the more I thought this is happening for a reason. This may be an opportunity, but for whom? So many questions raced through my mind. *Where has he been? Why didn't he ever apologize? What if he comes across my name the same way I came across his and tries to contact me? What can of worms have I just opened?!* Then a calming sensation came over me. I went back to the computer after madly pacing the floor. I sent him a friend request and just waited. The next day, he accepted. I now could see the face I hadn't seen since Lana died, the one that tormented me all these years, the boy that, in my mind, I turned into a monster. I'd never felt so power*ful* and power*less,* sitting in front of that computer screen. I looked at his profile and I saw him. Although now a man, that boyish face was still recognizable within the man's face. I felt sad for him, for me, for our families. We all had suffered so much. Suddenly, rather than revenge or fear, I felt I had to somehow tell him how sorry I was for everyone. I wanted to forgive him, but I had to make sure of a few things first.

To truly forgive him, I would have to be okay and accept whatever the outcome would be. There was a possibility that he wouldn't respond, that he had a wonderful life now, or that he might tell me to get over it, and piss off. Maybe he wasn't sorry or felt any responsibility. I had to be okay with whatever happened before I sent that email. This had to be strictly for me. I couldn't allow his response, whatever it would be, to nourish the seeds of anger. It took me a couple of days to be sure; then I sat down and wrote from my heart. I sent it without expectations, judgments, or hatred. I didn't know if he would respond, and it didn't matter.

Tim did respond. I feel that this exchange between us was one of the most revealing, healing things I've ever done. These are the actual letters between us, and I'm proud and honored to share them with you.

The longest letter I ever waited to write:

> *For thirteen years, I thought long and hard about what I might say to you if I ever had the opportunity. Here it is: There is no one person in this world that has ever touched my life so deeply without being in it. I hated you for a long time; I felt sorry for you at times and often wondered why you never reached out to me to say anything at all. I felt like you weren't sorry. It took a very long time for me to see that it didn't really matter how sorry or sad you were, ultimately, I am responsible for how I feel. I thought about telling you how utterly devastated my family was, and in some ways still is. I thought about making you aware of every memory and chance that was lost to me in part because of you. I'll admit I wanted you to suffer forever, like I thought I would. You*

made a poor choice that had devastating consequences when you were a young man. We all have changed. I've realized that all the moments that I thought you took from me with my sister were never mine. Everyone has their time and no one is guaranteed a long life. I have realized that the great suffering I endured has brought me the greatest gifts of my life. There is no one in this world who appreciates life, love and friendship as much as I do. I don't want you to suffer; I would never want anyone to go through what I have. I have no regrets for where this life has brought me. So thank you. I wish for you that you found forgiveness for yourself from that devastating event. I wish for you that you don't take anything in this life for granted. I wish for you that Lana inspired you to always be a better man, father, friend, son, brother for the rest of your life. I wish for you all the happiness that this life has to offer. If you need to, feel free to respond. For my own piece of mind, I wanted you to know that I have forgiven you.

Melanie

This is the letter I received in response from Tim:

Dear Melanie,

Well, I don't know where to begin. I'm sorry it took me a week to respond, my computer crashed. That wasn't the only reason. I didn't really know what to say. I've been thinking about it for years. But still, I never tried to contact you for two reasons. The first is selfish: I was scared to. The second was less selfish; I knew you hated me and I thought that might help you deal. I hated myself sometimes and that helped me for a few moments or so. I was at a friend's house in Uxbridge, Janelle, and she showed me her photo album and there you were. A few months later, I was running the Wallace in Port Perry, I think you came in. Then I didn't know what to say, but I'll give it my best shot now: I would do anything to change what happened. I loved Lana very much and would never have done anything to hurt her on purpose. I will never get over what happened, nor want to. I have moved on though. In November, my cousin, Aaron, drowned in Lake Scugog. He was the closest person to me in the world. We lived together, worked together and played together. Losing Lana is still hard on me. I know I'm not very good at letters. I want to say I'm sorry, but the words seem too small. If I can do anything to somehow make things easier, any questions you need answered. Anything I can do, please ask. As I said I'm really not good at writing letters, so again I'm sorry, if this one doesn't come out right, but I do promise it's from the heart.

Tim

Reaction: a reverse movement or tendency; an action in a reverse direction or manner. An action in response to some influence.

I was surprised at the reaction of the people close to me when I told them I was writing my letter. Some were very supportive, while others became really angry that I had chosen to forgive him. That didn't sway my decision at all. They were all very protective. Before, I relished the supportive anger of the group. I wanted to hear them tell me I was right to hate him, to justify my pain and outrage, to cheer me on in how awful this person must have been. Now, I could clearly see they were all suffering. Now, when I saw the hurt on their faces for me, it was not a hurtful reminder of my pain, but a reminder of their own. Now, looking back at the people who expressed their love to me, I could feel love for them. I was proud of myself to see how I had grown.

I thought that Tim was so far away all these years. As we began to talk, I found out that he also had travelled to Vancouver, lived in the town next to me, and knew several of the people I hung around. He had been living his life right next to mine all along. It was as if the universe or God was providing me with a million opportunities to find him, and offering me a way to let go of the heavy burden of pain that was crushing me. As soon as I forgave him, I stopped thinking about him. The enormous weight was lifted from me.

So many people said I was such a big person for doing that: for forgiving him. I never understood them. I never felt like there was any other choice. Or that it made me a good or better person. It just made me a freer person. I actually felt guilty for making him wait so long, to relieve him of his suffering. I couldn't be responsible any longer for making someone else suffer. I was trying to become more compassionate.

If you had told me I would have forgiven him after the accident, I would never have believed it. It took a lot of time to sort myself out. Although I have healed from Lana's death, even now, I still struggle with my depression. I am generally a very happy person, but there are dark days. I have been on at least half a dozen anti-depressants. I support anyone who finds them beneficial, but for me, as an extremely creative person, the drugs made me feel like I couldn't truly tap into that part of my personality anymore. I needed to find another way to deal with my depression. Those drugs were replaced with lots of vitamins, yoga and meditation.

I never forgot the meditation classes at the hospital. I signed up for yoga classes and practiced for ten years. It became my vehicle to sanity and brought me such peace and joy. I had a very special teacher, Penny, who saw a light in me and encouraged me in so many ways. She told me I needed to teach, and gave me a free pass to a very special yoga school in Toronto called "Esther Myers." I did a two-year, teacher-training program and have been teaching Yoga and Meditation ever since, drug-free. Not struggle-free, but I have the tools and faith now to understand my mind with more compassion. I am not suggesting if you are on medication, to stop taking it. I am only sharing what worked for me. I had three teachers at the yoga studio where I did my training. Tama, Paola and Monica, and they were three of the most inspirational, loving teachers I could have had. I remember the first time I met these women, they emanated such a peaceful energy about them. I was thinking to myself, *I don't know what these women are on, but I want some of whatever they got*. They were high on life. Now *that,* I could get addicted to. It was amazing. As soon as I heard them speak, I knew I was in the right place, and I knew that Penny knew me well enough to realize it too. Thank you Penn, my Yoga Angel. The training changed who I was. It challenged me not only physically, but spiritually and blessed me with so many gifts. It was a powerful awakening for me. I try to share my experiences with my students in the loving way my teachers shared their insights and wisdom with me.

A lot of time has passed since Lana's death. I often think to myself if she were here, just making an appearance right now, would she believe all the amazing things that happened since she left? Maybe a quick summary would go something like this:

> *Lana, here's the short version: Your best friend, Kelly, became one of my best friends, and I stood up for her at her wedding. She still makes me laugh harder than anyone. Kim married a cop, travelled the world, and is the best aunt in the world to my kids. Mike married and moved to Texas. Whenever I think of him, I miss him. Sonya came home after ten years in the Yukon and married the Coffee Shop guy. They have become two of my closest friends, and not just cause Craig is as crazy about music as I. Joanne had two boys and still works and drinks like a man. I made new friends too, whom I know you would love, like Carolyn and Tim, and Tammy and Dave. . Remember Kathleen? She had just as crazy a life as I, and was one of the inspirations for this book. Mom was married for a third time and still prays for us. She spoils the kids ridiculously. Dad bought a house and stayed sober at my wedding. I think we have a half sister too. Nanny and Pepere lived for a very long time, and were so proud of us. They adored my kids. Nanny had a huge crush on Jeff. I have a daughter who, in a lot of ways, is so much like you. She's clumsy and sarcastic and super-smart. I have a son who is just as fearless and fiery as you. Aunt Shirley does all the crazy things with the kids that she did with us: trips to N.B and special boxes for the kids in the mail. She calls almost every day.*

> *She's always excited for dinners at Teddy's when she comes to visit; she's our saint. Emerson died just like we thought he would. And as for me… Would you believe I got married to a country boy, moved out to a cottage town, became a yoga teacher, got a job at the local country market, and continue to write music, make CDs, and perform all over? Can you believe it? I wrote a book too, little sis, and I couldn't have* done it without you.

Every now and then, I think of all the things that have happened since she died. I don't look at it as the moments she's missed anymore, but how much life I have lived.

Chapter 9: Awakenings

Awakening: awaking from sleep, revival of interest or attention. A recognition, realization, or coming into awareness of something.

We always think that the most important relationships are the ones that we invested the most time into. For me, I realize now that every relationship, short or long, can have a lasting impact on the people we are and whom we become. We can take a piece of every new person we meet and carry it with us. Whether it is a simple bowl of soup or teaching someone a song on the piano, these moments can be the purest form of true friendship and healing. I learned that we don't just have one soul mate; there are many souls that connect us and teach us throughout our lives, and all are deeply meaningful. We just need to have our hearts and eyes open to find the priceless significance that exists in every person. Every person has something of value to offer.

In the moment of crisis, it was hard for me to see how important all these events were, and to find any meaning in them. It took many years and many more travails for me to figure it out. I still don't have it all figured out. The whole reason for this book was not to tell you a sad story, but to share with you what I have discovered on my journey. I hope that it may inspire or teach you something about your own life.

In this life, we expect a lot of things to happen; we feel like certain things are owed to us. Things like a long life, watching our friends and family grow and get married, having their own families, achieving all their dreams, and fulfilling all the important milestones that this life has to offer. It's arrogant and naïve. I once knew of a boy with a serious illness. When asked, "Do you ever ask God why this happened to you?"

He answered, so confidently, "Why not me?"

I thought that was so profound. I spent a very long time saying things like: "My sister never got to be an aunt, my sister never went to her prom, my sister never got married…" like these events and experiences were somehow owed to me and then snatched away. It comes down to what is our purpose here? Life is the school. Everyone has good and bad things that happen to him or her. Every second, we have a choice to find the meaning, to learn from, and about ourselves, to become better. When we get better and find joy and happiness, we fill ourselves up, and when we are full, we have a lot to share. I don't know why some people find a way to see past pain, and others keep running in painful circles. It seems like there is a moment, a game changer that allows some of us to rise above the traumatic events of our lives.

I wish I could offer an answer. It took me getting pregnant to really begin to use the tools I was given at the hospital and through therapy. It was also the people and friends I found who made it possible for me to grow and heal. I believe as humans, we need each other. We need these intimate connections with other people to find our true purpose here. Those moments, those game changers are waiting for us to just open our eyes and see them. The truth is: my sister was never meant to be an aunt, or get married, or graduate. She was here for the time she was given, and she turned out to be a great teacher for many people in her short life. Her life was no less meaningful because she died. It makes her life that much more precious. By recognizing this, I can truly honor her memory. We can't go back, but we can try to be the best we can be right now, and then the future is always taken care of. I think Buddha said that.

The day my sister died was the best and worst day of my life. You might wonder how I could see it as one of the best things to happen to me. It tore out my soul, and made me question everything I had ever believed about this life. I truly hit the bottom of myself. Not everyone can say they've had that opportunity. Yes, I said opportunity. It is wonderful to wipe the slate clean, and to start deciding for oneself what to believe in, for no one else, but oneself. There is freedom in not trying to please anyone else or be swayed or influenced by anyone else's perceptions. That's not to say that we don't need other people to guide us, or influence us in a positive light. For me, I had to reconstruct all of my core values and what I wanted out of this life. I had to decide who I wanted to be, and how I saw myself. Once I arrived at my careful decision of what I could handle, and what I needed, then the influences and people in my life became something that enriched me. It was empowering to accept advice without feeling obligated to obey it. To use what connected with me, what worked for my life, instead of doing something because I didn't want to disappoint others.

Some people spend their whole lives not knowing what they believe in, or not being confident in the decisions they make for themselves. It's not enough just to be confident in making decisions. We are all human and prone to making wrong choices. Confidence lies in being able to handle whatever the outcome or the consequences may be.

For me, it was learning to accept the bad things that happen, and understanding that I can make mistakes without losing sight of my purpose. I wanted to use my experiences and tools to hopefully handle my own crises with more grace, and even possibly help others. It took many more years to trust myself and my decisions and be confident that I would always handle, to the best of my ability, all of life's great challenges. It's a lifelong process.

My breakdown at first forced me to listen. At times, throughout this journey, I was so spent, there was nothing left to do but listen. I learned that you didn't always have to have the right answers for someone, but just being present was very often the answer itself. If only my hospital friends knew what great teachers they were.

There was something amazing that I discovered about birth and death. For me, they were the only occasions in my life where time truly stood still. In those moments, nothing else mattered. You don't care what time it is or what clothes you're wearing, or what's for dinner. You are completely present in the silence, in your pain, and in a way, that is a beautiful thing. I remember once driving to a friend's funeral and looking out the window of the car. The sun was shining in my eyes, the sky was blue and birds were flying by. I thought to myself how incredibly beautiful it was at that moment. My mind wasn't racing, I wasn't distracted. I was completely present to see these things, to really see them despite my suffering. It was instantaneous. To be still and present like that, to recognize that sensation of instant joy without any judgments, thoughts, or preconceptions.

We have this amazing gift of opportunity to honor our loved ones with that kind of wholeheartedness.

The Water Drop Connection

What "The Water Drop Connection" means, and why I chose this title.

I once read that this is a saying in Burma, which I thought was incredibly beautiful. For me, during this challenging time in my life, it was the people around me who helped me come through. Some of those friendships were very brief, and some have stayed with me for life. But they all had importance and value in my healing process. To this day, my friends and people around me continue to inspire me to strive harder and try to be a better person. I can't imagine my life without my friends. And I can't imagine living my life without going out into the world to make new ones.

In Burma, there is an expression that describes sacred friendship. "Yezed sounde" means: "water drop connection." It describes the experience of meeting someone and feeling an immediate connection. It's like these two people combine and become one, like water droplets, running down a smooth surface. There is a movement of mental and physical forces that exists in ceaseless flow from moment to moment, and life to life. Burmese people believe that "In some past life, I did something good for you, and you did something good for me, or we performed skillful actions together for the benefit of others." Pure friendship of this kind kindles a feeling of recognition and a sense of "being recognized."

The power of sacred friendship is not only a catalyst for awakening to truth, it also heals, empowers, and liberates. When we see with the eyes of compassion and understanding, we can begin the long and rewarding journey of accepting all the diverse and fragmented pieces of our psyche, and we discover the goodness within ourselves.

My story is about the many sacred friendships that I have been blessed with in my life. It is with gratitude and love that I acknowledge all the wonderful beings who have lit my path, supported me and taught me everything so far. I look forward to the many more friends, whom I'm sure to meet along the way. I hope this book and sharing my journey will allow you to look at me as not just an author, or a girl who suffered greatly and overcame her loss, but a sacred friend who helped light your path in some way.

I breathe in at this beautiful, wonderful and complicated life.

I breathe out and smile at complicated.

Thank you, Thich Nhat Hanh

Namaste

Melanie J. Hebert

www.ingramcontent.com/pod-product-compliance
Ingram Content Group UK Ltd.
Pitfield, Milton Keynes, MK11 3LW, UK
UKHW041918190726
13854UKWH00003B/1307